# THE BROONS GUIDE TAE
## *Family Planning*

# THE BROONS GUIDE TAE
## *Family Planning*

BLACK & WHITE PUBLISHING

First published 2017
by Black & White Publishing Ltd
104 Commercial Street, Edinburgh, EH6 6NF

1 3 5 7 9 10 8 6 4 2      17 18 19 20

ISBN: 978 1 910230 46 6


Text by Euan Kerr and Black & White Publishing
www.thebroons.com



A CIP catalogue record for this book is available from the British Library.

Typeset by Creative Link, North Berwick
Printed and bound by Opolgraf, Poland

Maw and Paw Broon have had eight children of wide-ranging ages. They've had so many offspring that they ran out of names for them and ended up having to call their youngest simply the Bairn. If you're planning a family, let this book be a guide and warning to you.

Having a large family can be wonderful, but when the menfolk suggested that it would be good to have another three male children in the family so that they could make up two five-a-side teams, the ladies didn't seem too enamoured by the idea.

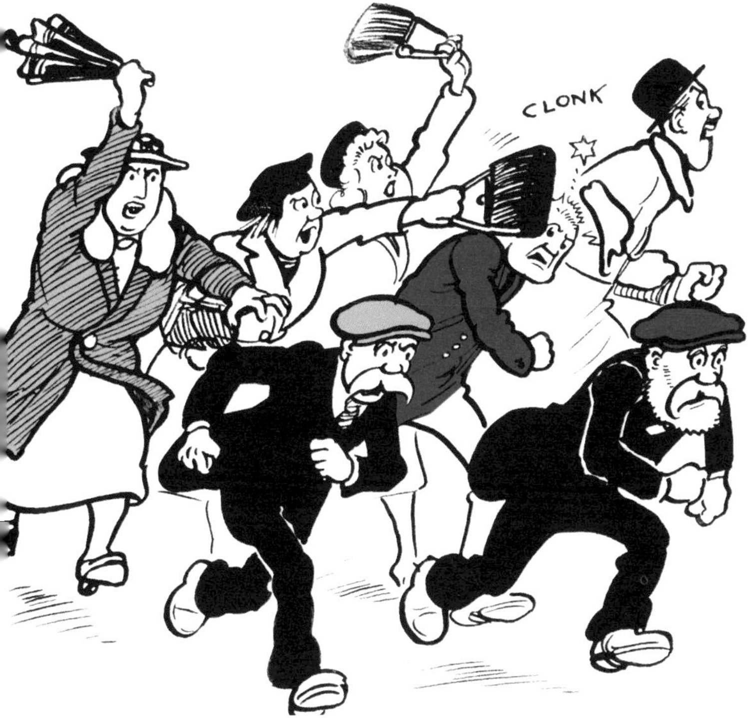
CLONK

Maw always wanted more girls and this became particularly clear when she used to give the boys rather feminine presents.

The Easter bonnets were bad enough, but can you imagine Joe in a frilly nightie?

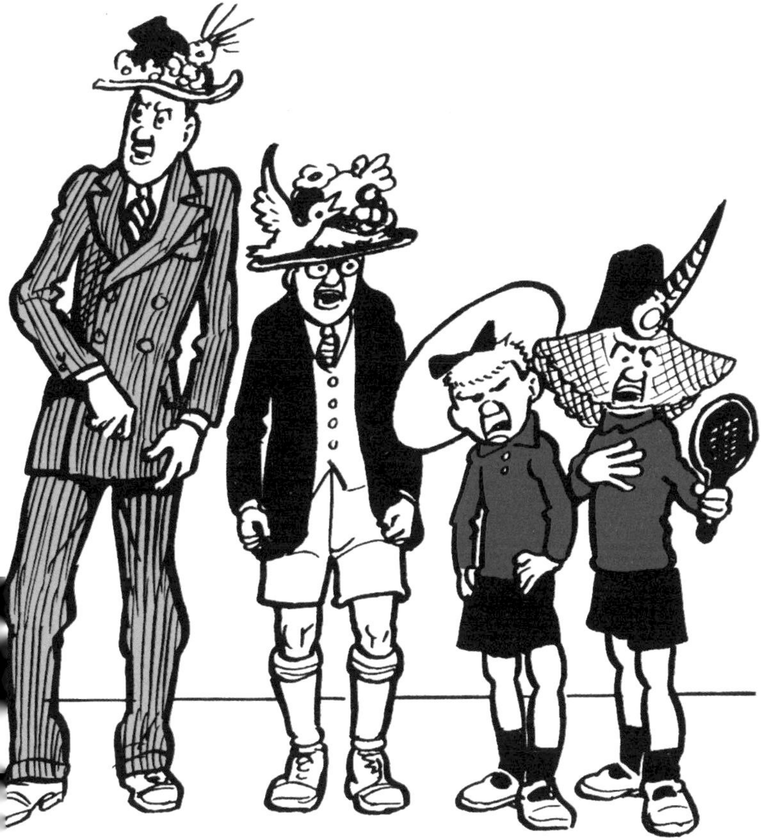

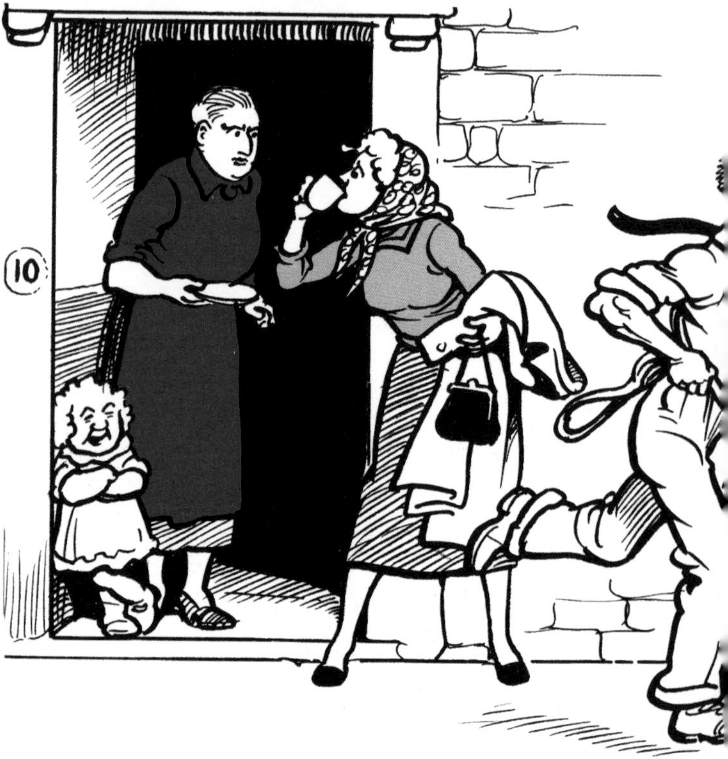
10

Mornings can be a nightmare trying to get everybody ready for work and school. You tend to put on the first clothes you can grab and run out the door.

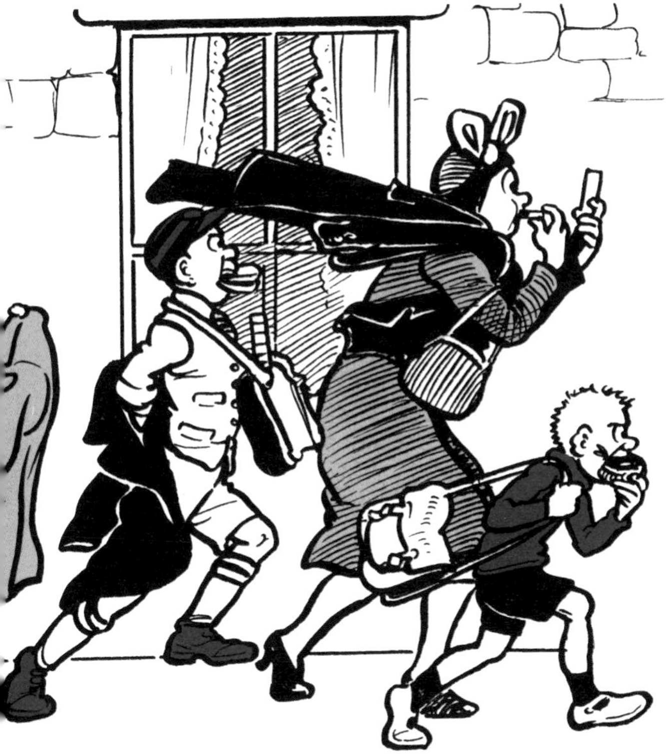

It's not the first time Paw's spent the day in Daphne's bloomers. He found them surprisingly comfortable but didn't like how Daph stretched his Y-fronts.

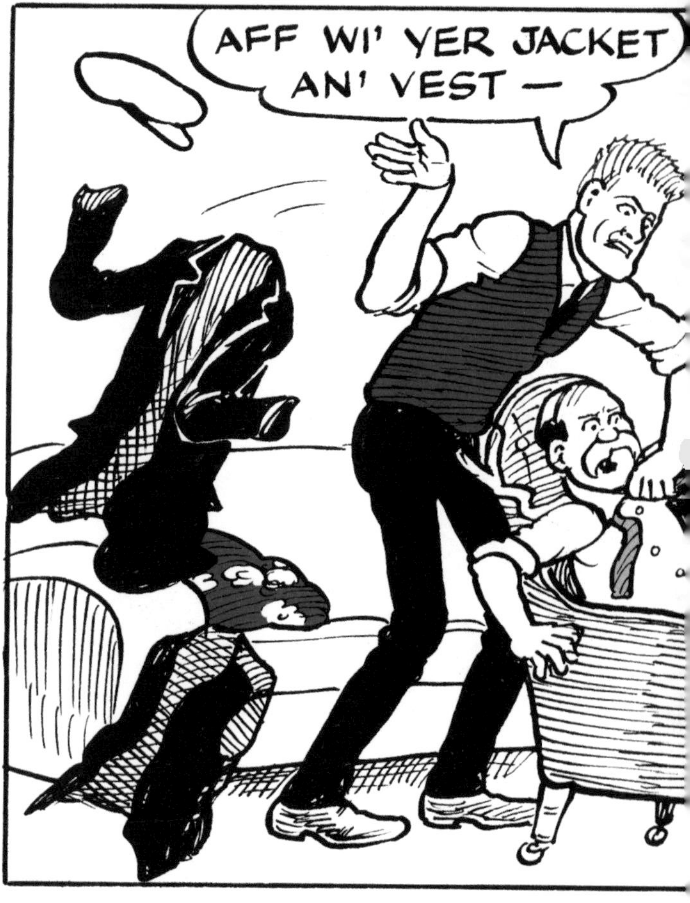
AFF WI' YER JACKET AN' VEST —

Getting outfits for all the family can be a problem. Sometimes Hen and Joe are so short of clothes that they have to

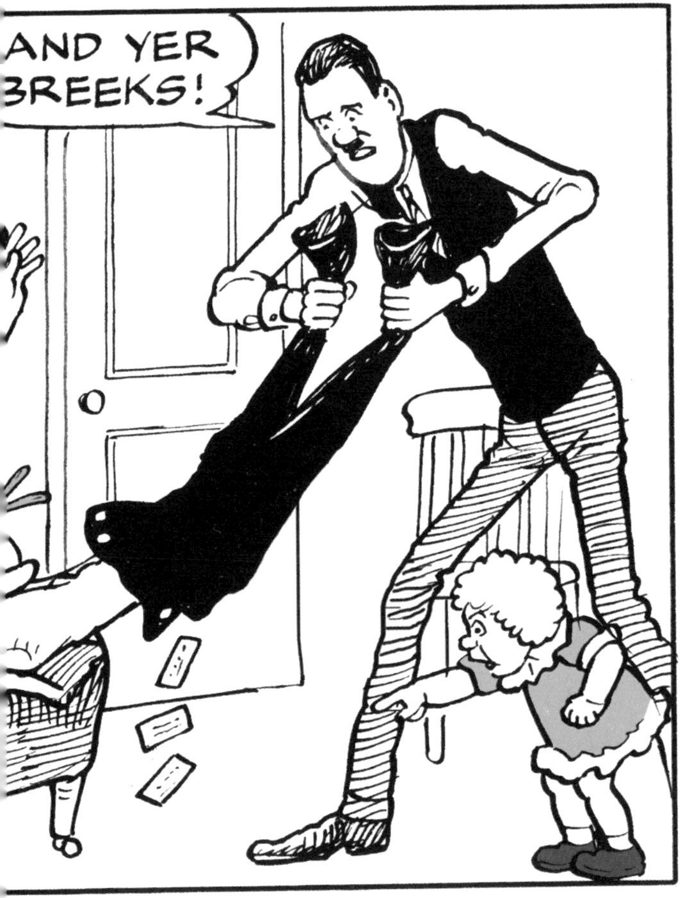
AND YER BREEKS!

'borrow' Paw's. Not a bad fit for Joe, but Paw's trousers look like long shorts on Hen. They do both forego the 'bunnet'.

It's a nightmare when the Broons get visitors. They don't have enough seats to go round. Sometimes Hen, Joe and Paw have to put chair covers over themselves so that there are enough seats for everyone. This can cause some embarrassing situations.

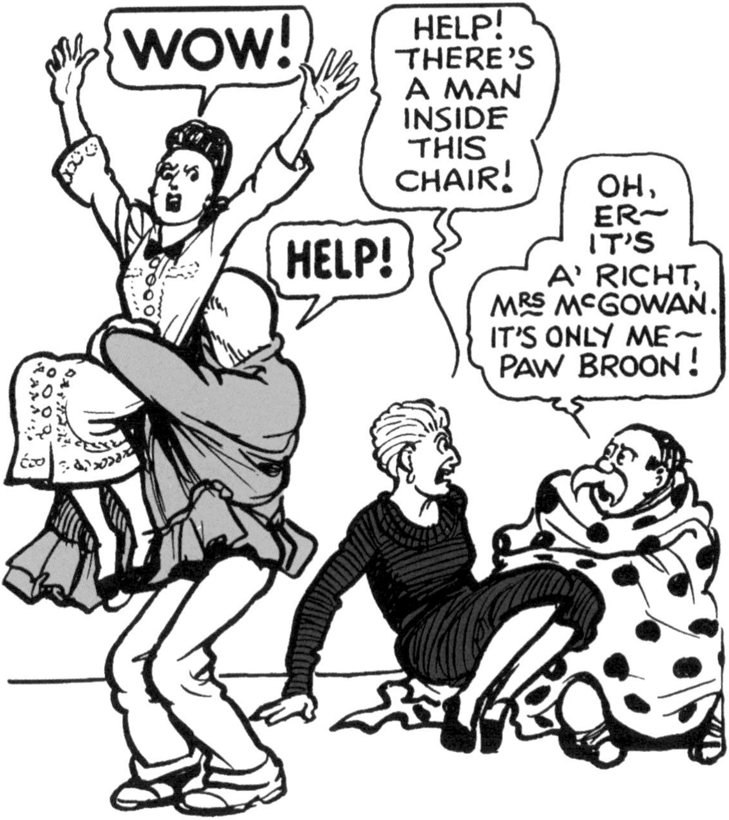
WOW!
HELP!
HELP! THERE'S A MAN INSIDE THIS CHAIR!
OH, ER~ IT'S A' RICHT, MRS McGOWAN. IT'S ONLY ME~ PAW BROON!

There are always petty sibling rivalries in big families. The girls are the worst. This wasn't the first time Maggie tried to drown her sister Daphne when she thought she was making eyes at one of her boyfriends.

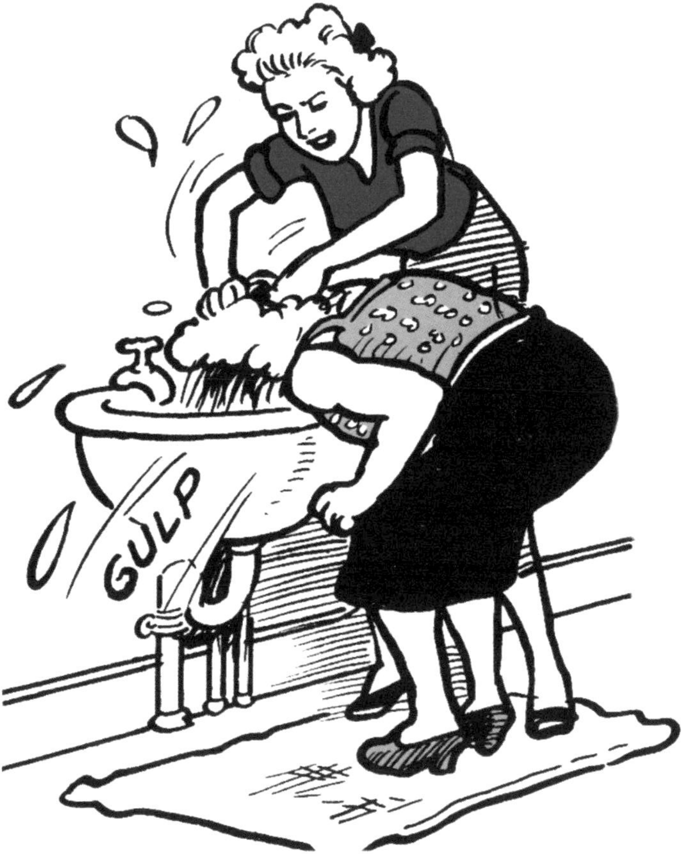
GULP

Hen tends to take Maggie's side too. Poor Daphne has a terrible time of it. The Bairn doesn't help by encouraging her big brother. The little scamp! It took two hours with a scrubbing brush to get Daphne clean again.

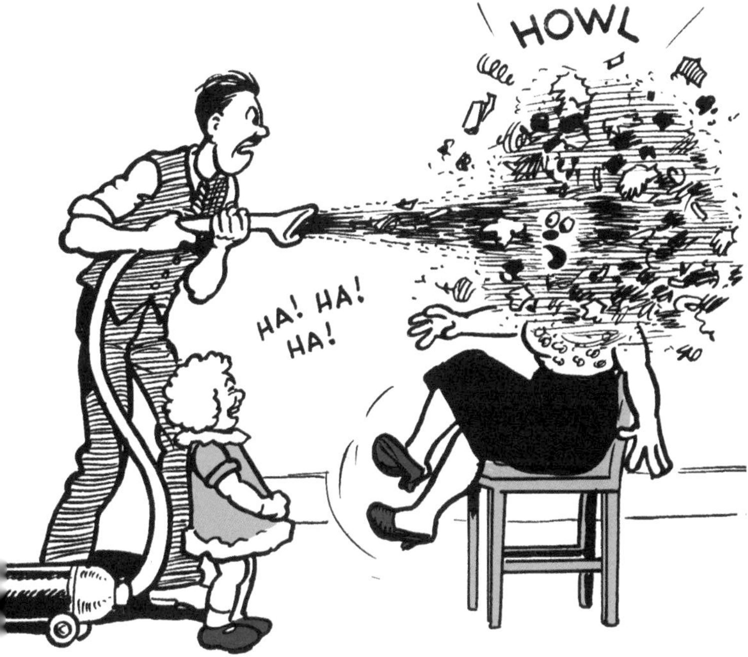
HOWL
HA! HA! HA!

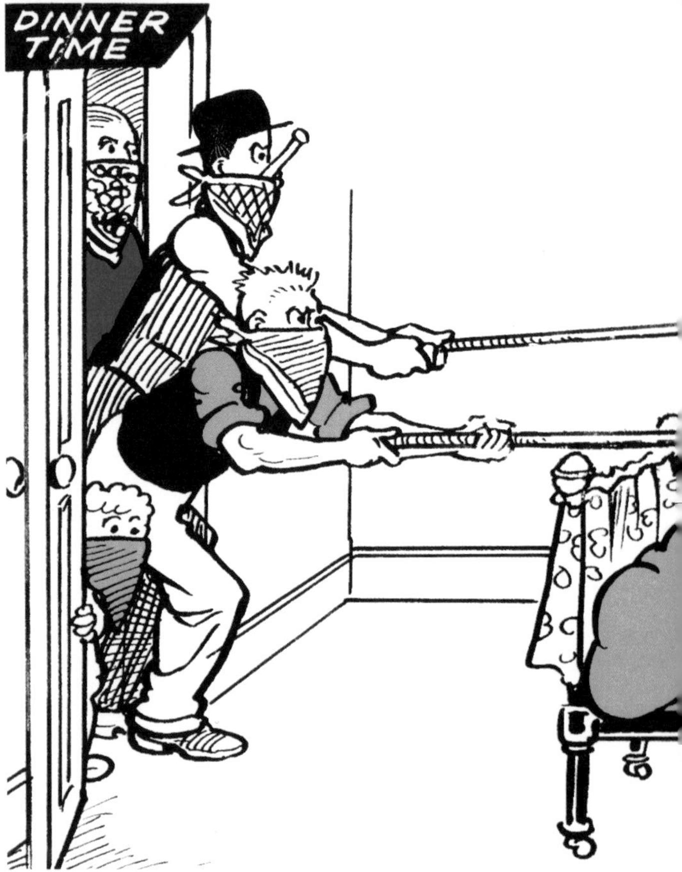
DINNER TIME

Another perennial problem of large families is socks. There's just not enough to go round and Paw's worn the same pair

Gran'paw handed down to him
in 1943. They're a bit whiffy
now and the family sometimes
refuse to go anywhere near him.

None of the family have ever left home. This could well be because of Maw's fantastic cooking. Not all her dishes have been winners, however, and the results of her cauliflower and sprout curry had devastating effects on poor old Paw's trousers.

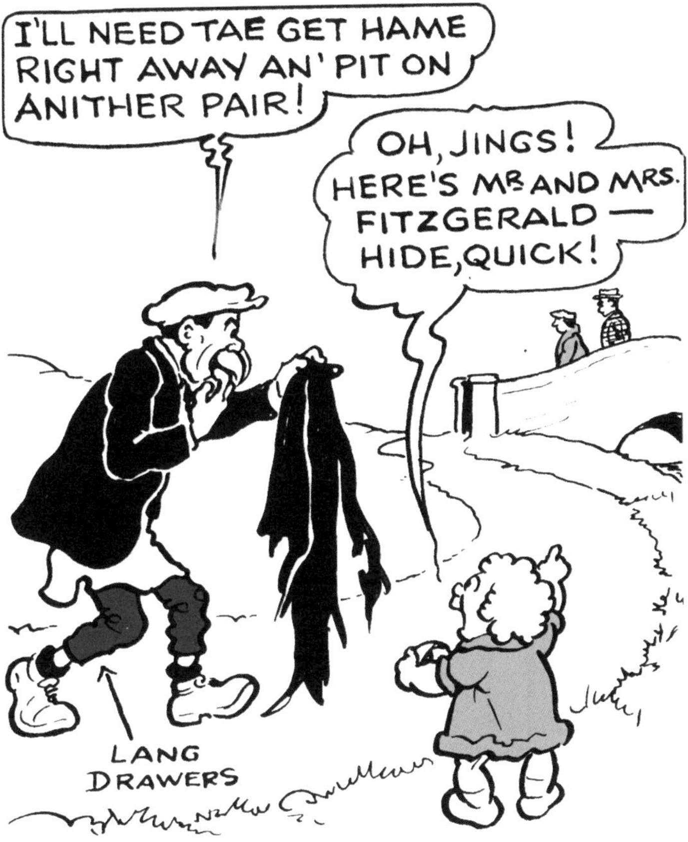
I'LL NEED TAE GET HAME RIGHT AWAY AN' PIT ON ANITHER PAIR!
OH, JINGS! HERE'S MR AND MRS. FITZGERALD — HIDE, QUICK!
LANG DRAWERS

With one bathroom and four women in the house, it could be a nightmare for the men to get clean. Sometimes they would hurl insults at the woman down the street just so they could get a shower.

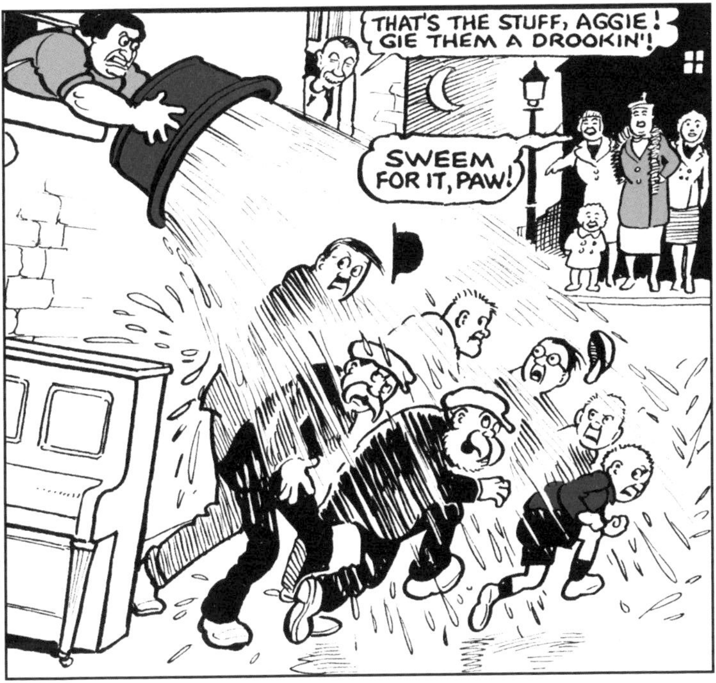
THAT'S THE STUFF, AGGIE! GIE THEM A DROOKIN'!
SWEEM FOR IT, PAW!

Having a large family can be a lot of fun – but not for poor Paw when Hen and Joe tricked him into believing they had the perfect cure for hiccups. This involved a funnel and some icy water. It did shock him into stopping hiccupping but he'd have probably rather kept the hiccups.

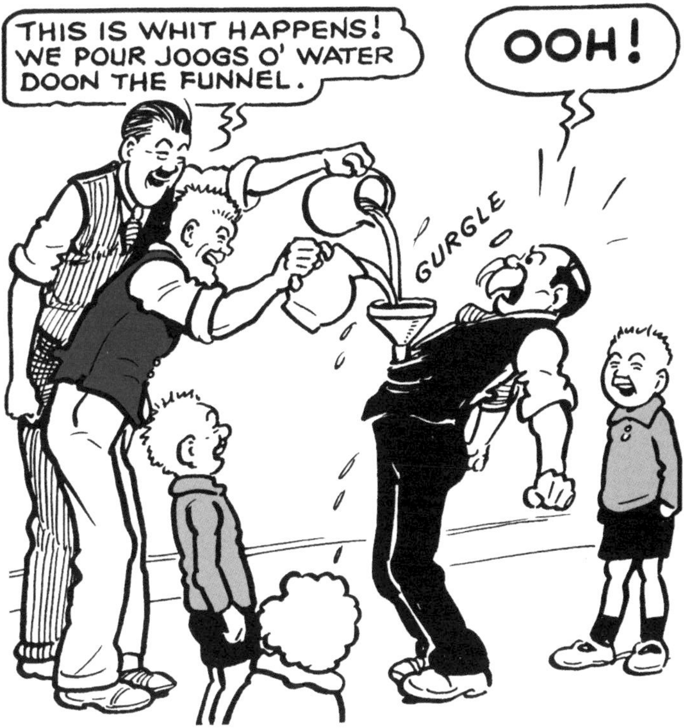
THIS IS WHIT HAPPENS! WE POUR JOOGS O' WATER DOON THE FUNNEL.
OOH!
GURGLE

Because Hen's so tall, he keeps on banging his head off low branches, doorframes, etc. It has made him prone to flights of fancy. Sometimes he thinks he's an ostrich. Maw would take him to the doctor, but the eggs come in really handy.

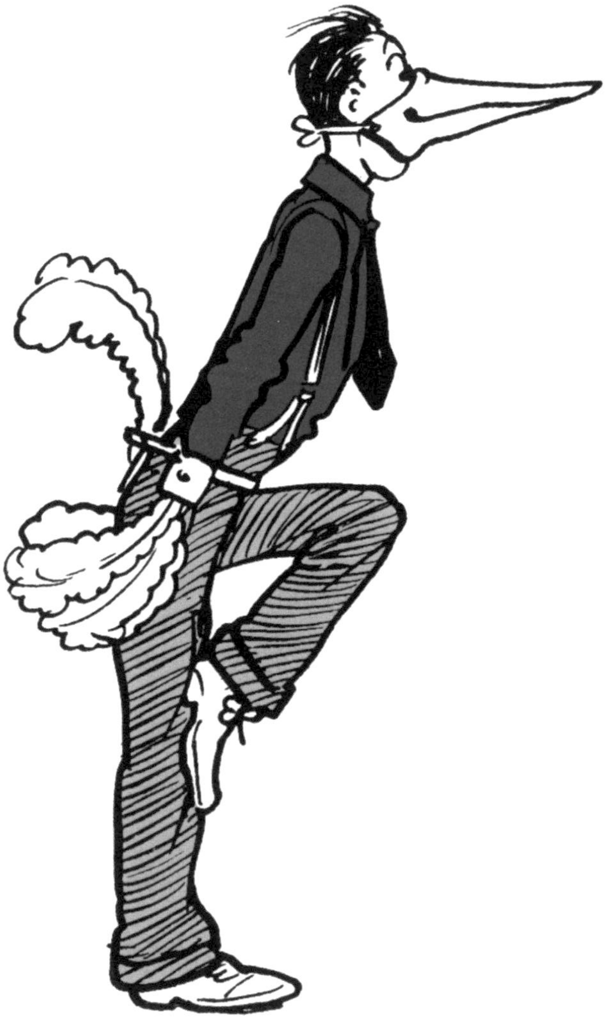

Sunshine holidays are
too expensive for ten of a
family but Paw convinces
the neighbours that the kids
have been to Majorca by
spraying them with treacle.
Inexpensive but messy!

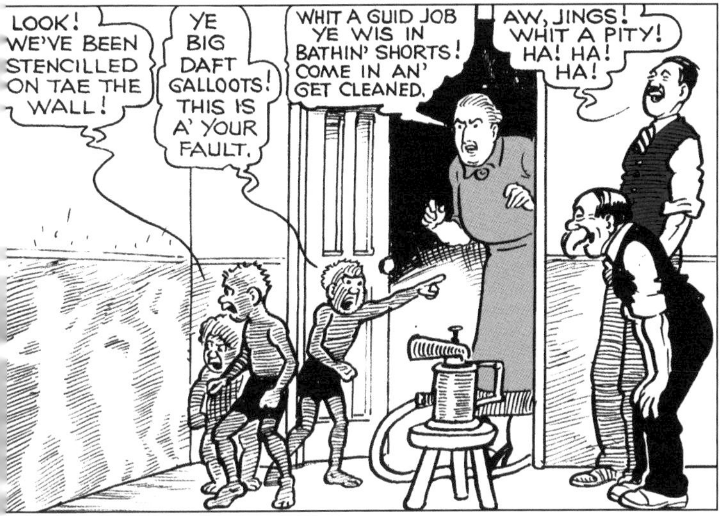
LOOK! WE'VE BEEN STENCILLED ON TAE THE WALL!
YE BIG DAFT GALLOOTS! THIS IS A' YOUR FAULT.
WHIT A GUID JOB YE WIS IN BATHIN' SHORTS! COME IN AN' GET CLEANED.
AW, JINGS! WHIT A PITY! HA! HA! HA!

Paw often worries that his younger offspring will struggle to find jobs when they're older. To that end, he is training the Twins in the building trade and has hopes that the Bairn will learn tricks for *Britain's Got Talent.*

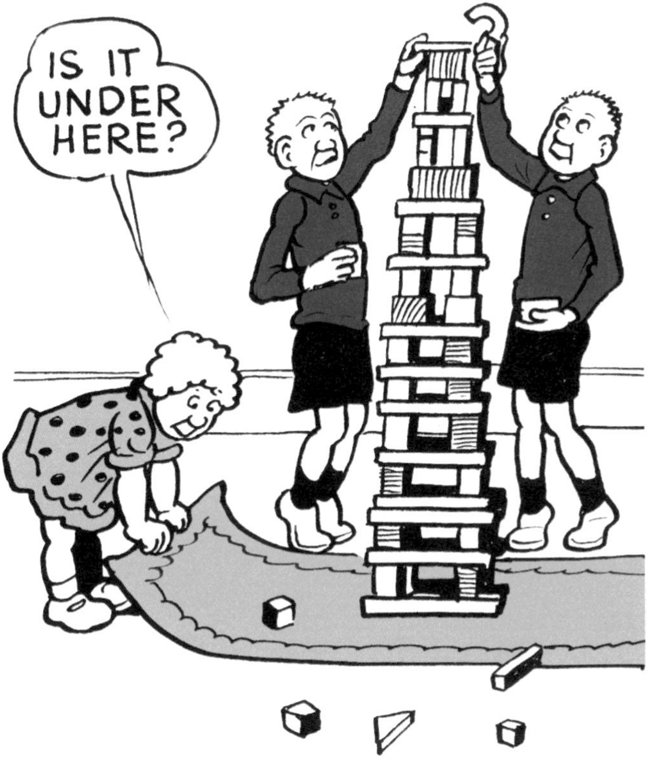
IS IT UNDER HERE?

To earn their keep, Maw and Paw are keen that the children form a family musical act to rival the Jackson Five, the Osmonds and the Bee Gees. Looks like the Broons Balladeers have a bit to go.

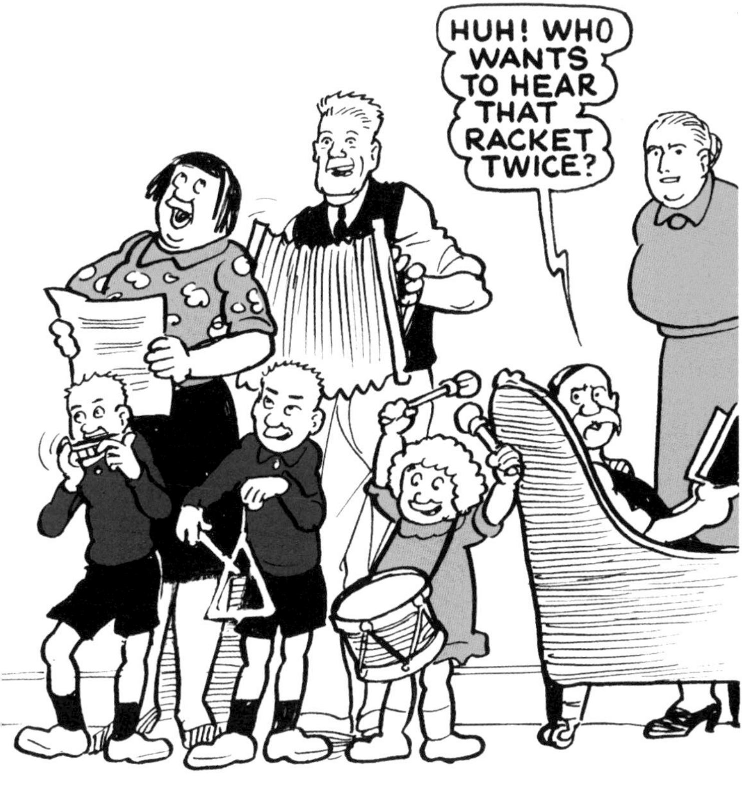
HUH! WHO WANTS TO HEAR THAT RACKET TWICE?

There is so much stuff left lying around in the Broons' house that Gran'paw has taken to clearing it up and selling it on eBay. As you see his 'cart is full' and he is about to 'proceed to checkout'.

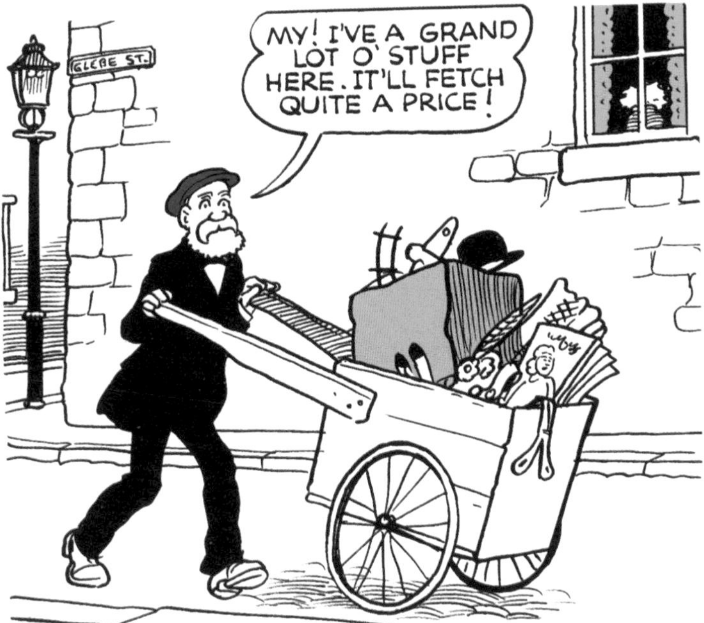
GLEBE ST.
MY! I'VE A GRAND LOT O' STUFF HERE. IT'LL FETCH QUITE A PRICE!

Sometimes money got really tight with having such a large family. There was the time when the Broons were all invited to Cousin Dougal's wedding. Once the ladies were kitted out, the menfolk only had enough money to hire one kilt.

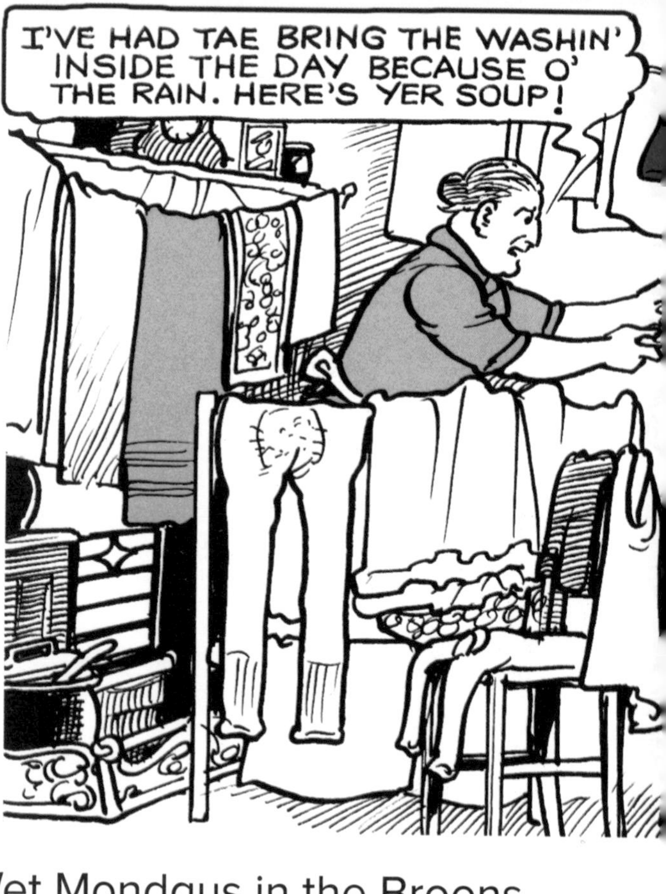
I'VE HAD TAE BRING THE WASHIN' INSIDE THE DAY BECAUSE O' THE RAIN. HERE'S YER SOUP!

Wet Mondays in the Broons household were no fun at all. Maw always did her washing on a Monday and, if it was raining, the wet clothes would be hung

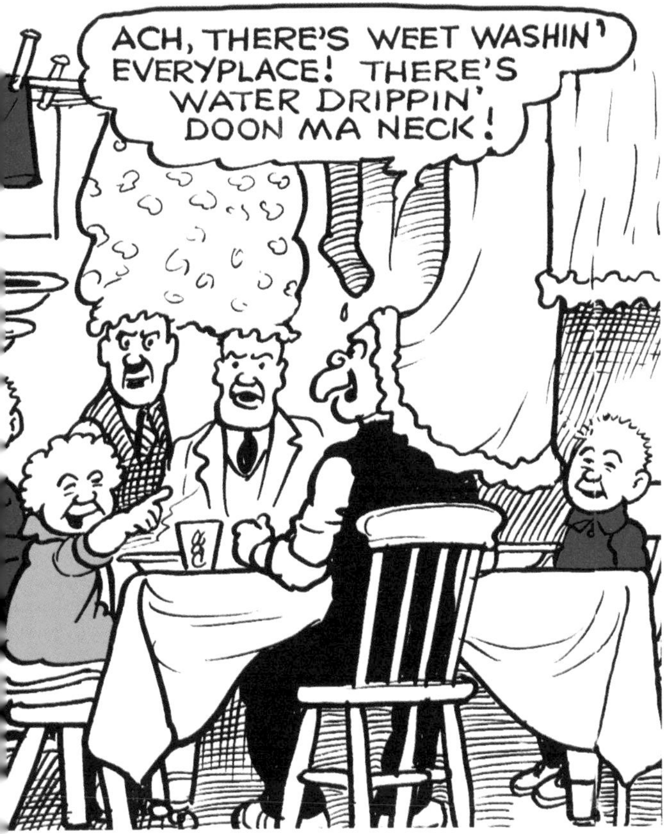
ACH, THERE'S WEET WASHIN' EVERYPLACE! THERE'S WATER DRIPPIN' DOON MA NECK!

up all over the house. With all that dampness and the fire blazing, 10 Glebe Street was like the Amazonian Rain Forest.

Sometimes the pressure of coping with such a large family has a very strange effect on Paw. There was the dreadful incident when he covered his head in whipped cream and imagined that he was a lorry driver. There was an almighty crash and Paw lost his No Claims Bonus.

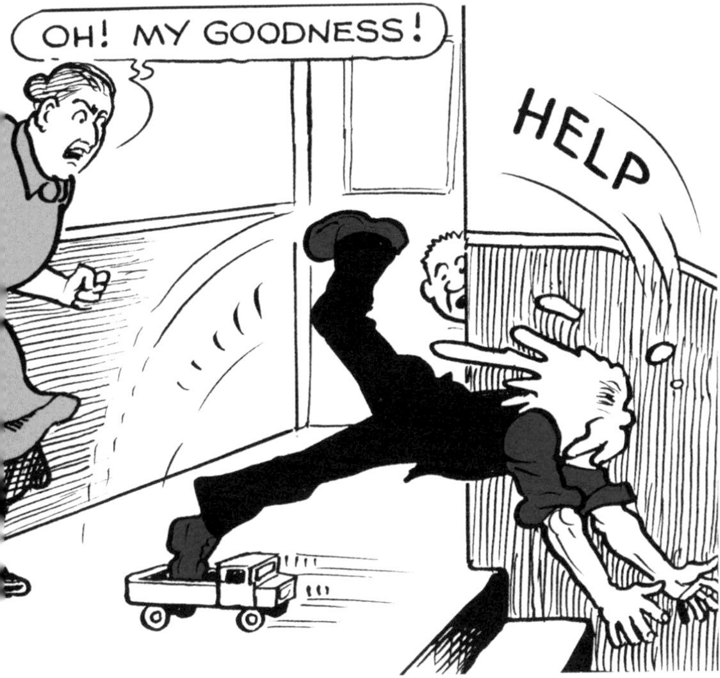
OH! MY GOODNESS!
HELP

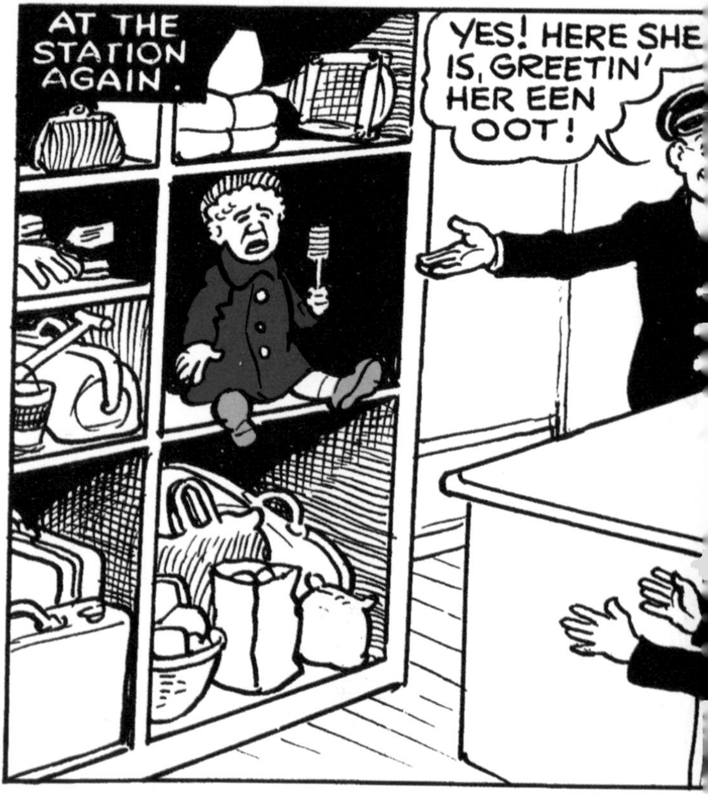
AT THE STATION AGAIN.
YES! HERE SHE IS, GREETIN' HER EEN OOT!

Paw's ashamed to admit that he has so many children, that he sometimes 'accidentally' leaves one or two behind.

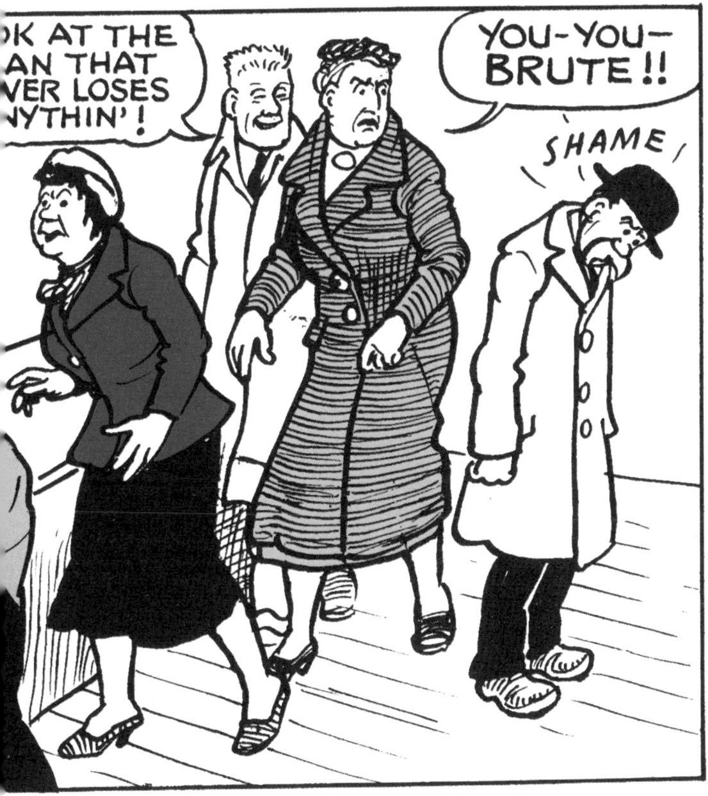
K AT THE
AN THAT
VER LOSES
YTHIN' !
YOU-YOU-
BRUTE !!
SHAME

Fortunately, they always seem to turn up somewhere or other.

Paw will do anything for his children. Honestly, the things he does for them! With Maw being a larger woman, he is the only one close enough to Maggie's size to act as a model when Maw and Daphne want to make a surprise new dress.

Hen tried to boost the family income by inventing the mains-linked waterbed. Unfortunately, during testing, there was a serious malfunction. However, the Twins didn't mind – they had great fun sailing their toy boats.

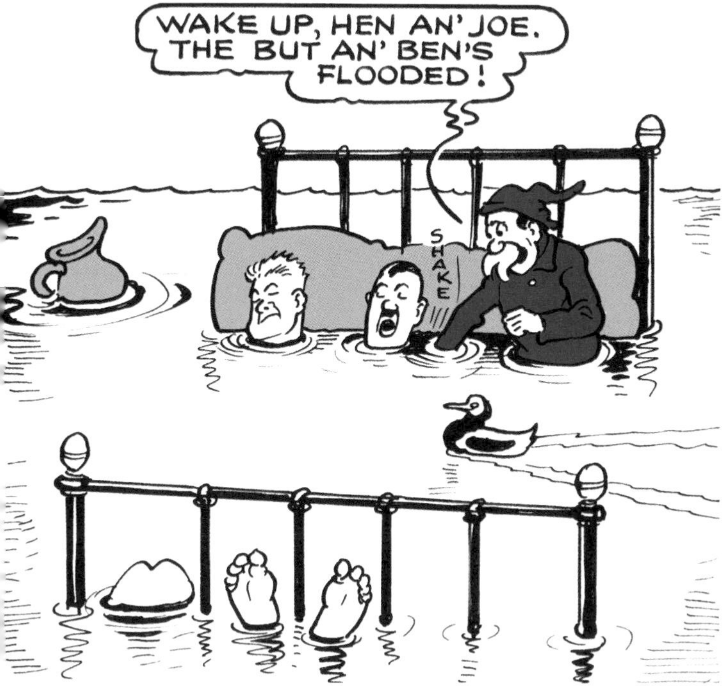
WAKE UP, HEN AN' JOE. THE BUT AN' BEN'S FLOODED!
SHAKE

Feuds within a large family are commonplace. Fed up with Paw always hogging the best fireside seat, Hen and Joe decided on retribution. They climbed onto the roof with a set of bellows and gave their father a mighty blast of smoke for being so selfish.

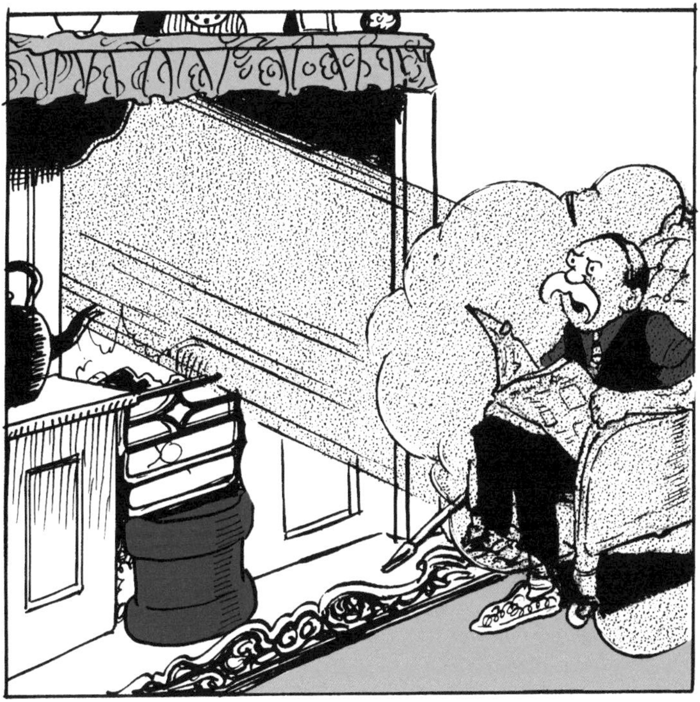

In an effort to supplement the family income, Maggie and Daphne decided to start a part-time dog-grooming business. Nanky Poo, the next door's Pekinese, was their first victim. They bathed him in exotic oils and perfume. The neighbourhood cats were delighted – they could smell the little brute sneaking up on them from half a mile away.

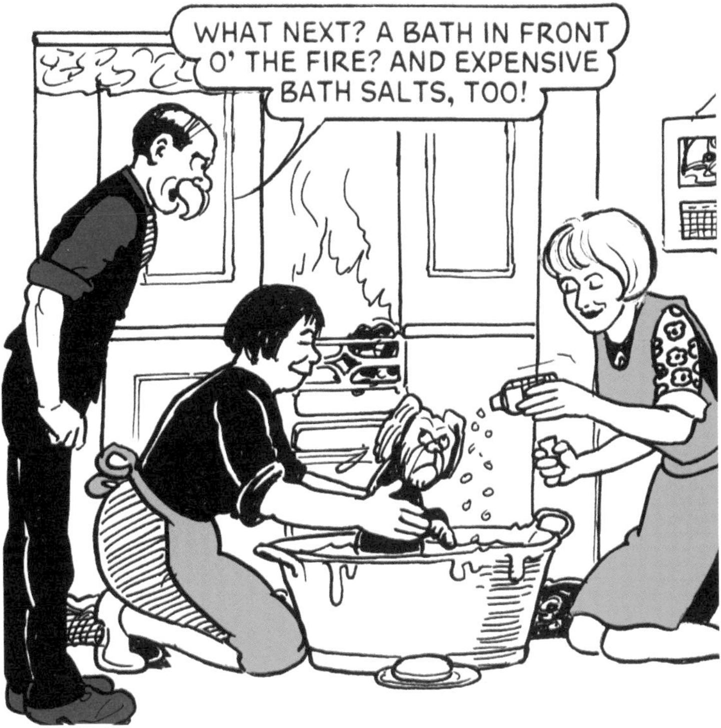
WHAT NEXT? A BATH IN FRONT O' THE FIRE? AND EXPENSIVE BATH SALTS, TOO!

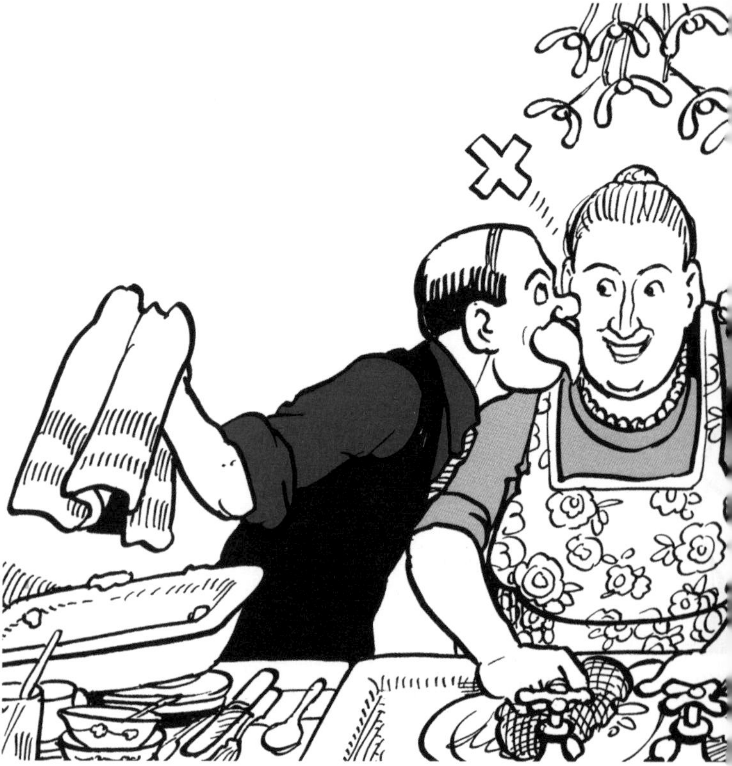

It's always difficult to get quality time together when there are so many children in the house. However, Maw and Paw always

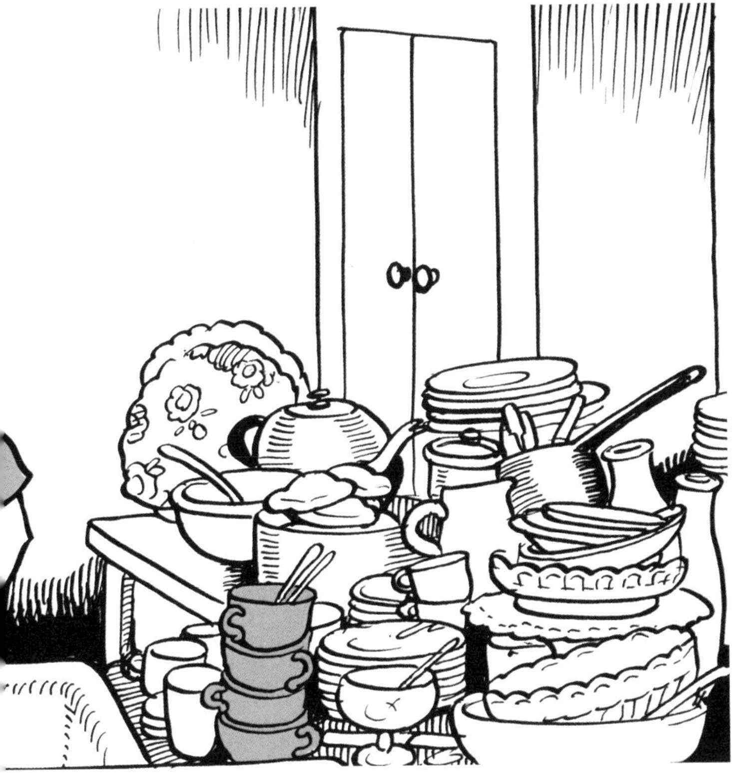

find that the family disappear sharpish when there is a pile of dishes needing done.

Families should always look after their old folk. In an effort to embarrass his family for not inviting him round for a Christmas meal, Gran'paw

pretended that he was so
lonely that the only guest he
could get for Christmas Dinner
was a turkey.

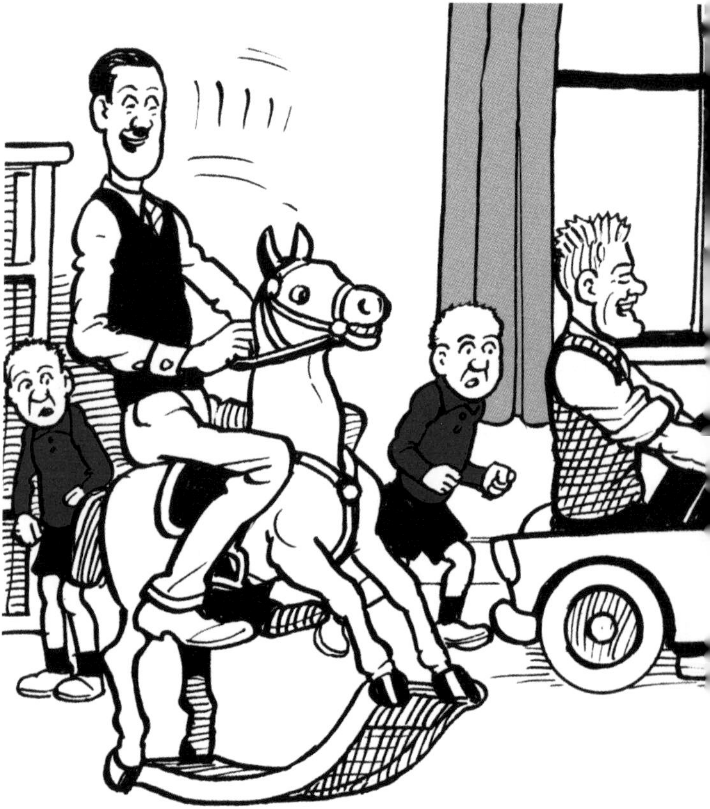

Hen and Joe had some very childish tendencies. Playing on the Twins' toys was bad enough but Maw and Paw grew

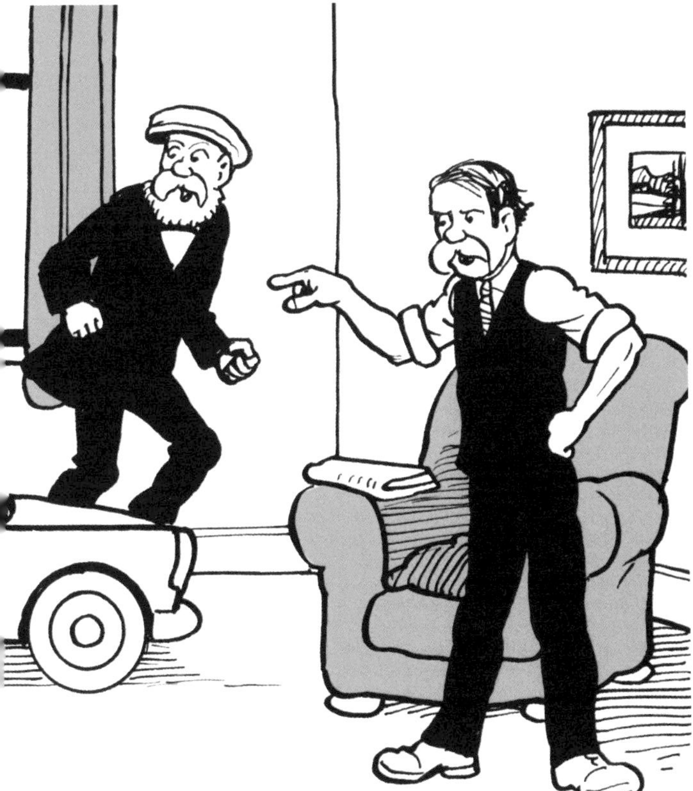

concerned with Joe's thumb sucking and Hen wearing a nappy.

Getting original presents for family members can be difficult. The Bairn gave Hen a REALLY original one this year – a bucket (which she borrowed from Oor Wullie) for washing the car she's going to buy him when she wins the lottery, which she's not allowed to play for umpteen years.

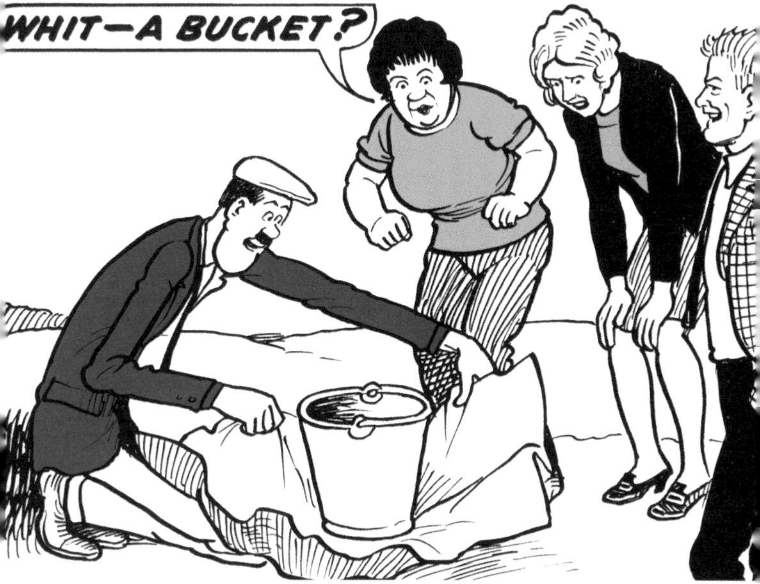
WHIT—A BUCKET?

So, why on earth did the Broons decide to have such a large family? Well, there are advantages in having a houseful of Broons. Five adults, all earning, four children bringing in a fortune in Child

Benefit and, of course, Maw's considerable earnings from the royalties on *Maw Broon's Cookbook* — how else do you think they can afford their 'country estate' a.k.a. the But an' Ben?

Paw wishes you the best of
luck in planning a family.
You'll need it . . .